# The Herd Keeper

by

*Alberto Caeiro*

# *Pessoa by Me* Collection

Volume 1

Cover: Photo by Pixabay "Birds flying on a Golden Sky" from Pexel

Source for text in Portuguese: http://arquivopessoa.net/

# The Herd Keeper

A Pagan Portuguese Poem

By Fernando Pessoa writing as Alberto Caeiro

Translated by Erick Messias 2023 ©

| | |
|---|---|
| Introducing Pessoa by Me | 8 |
| Introducing Alberto Caeiro | 10 |
| 1 | 14 |
| 2 | 18 |
| 3 | 20 |
| 4 | 22 |
| 5 | 24 |
| 6 | 28 |
| 7 | 30 |
| 8 | 32 |
| 9 | 38 |
| 10 | 40 |
| 11 | 42 |
| 12 | 44 |
| 13 | 46 |
| 14 | 48 |
| 15 | 50 |
| 15a | 52 |
| 16 | 54 |
| 17 | 56 |
| 18 | 58 |
| 19 | 60 |
| 20 | 62 |
| 21 | 64 |
| 22 | 66 |
| 23 | 68 |
| 24 | 70 |

| | |
|---|---|
| 25 | 72 |
| 26 | 74 |
| 27 | 76 |
| 28 | 78 |
| 29 | 80 |
| 30 | 82 |
| 31 | 84 |
| 32 | 86 |
| 33 | 90 |
| 34 | 92 |
| 35 | 94 |
| 36 | 96 |
| 37 | 98 |
| 38 | 100 |
| 39 | 102 |
| 40 | 104 |
| 41 | 106 |
| 42 | 108 |
| 43 | 110 |
| 44 | 112 |
| 45 | 114 |
| 46 | 116 |
| 47 | 120 |
| 48 | 122 |
| 49 | 124 |
| About the authors: Fernando Pessoa - One and Many | 126 |
| About the authors: Alberto Caeiro, the Poetic Sage of Simplicity | 128 |

About this translation.................................................. 130

## Introducing Pessoa by Me

Something surprised me when I first read or heard about Fernando Pessoa while in America. The great poet was known mostly by his prose volume known as The Book of Disquiet. The great poems cited included "Salutation to Walt Whitman" and "Maritime Ode."

Where was the poet and the poets, Caeiro, Campos and Reis? And where were lines such as "the poet is a sham" or "I am nothing, I will never be but nothing. I can't wish but to be nothing. Aside from this, I have in me every dream in the world" or "To be great, be whole" or "To think of God is to disobey God," - lines that I could find in my memory after all those years?

I then realized that to bring the Pessoa that populated my adolescence imagination I would have to look for those poems myself and thus this collection was created.

This is not an academic exercise, this is not professional translation, this is a work of love and *Saudade.* This is a way to introduce a Pessoa I met and left deep marks in my existence to my American children and friends. This is a way to collect the poems I encountered as an adolescent in Fortaleza in the 1990s and that have been with me since.

          Erick Leite Maia de Messias

# Introducing Alberto Caeiro

Fernando Pessoa has been called the "Portuguese Walt Whitman" by the literary critic Howard Bloom who included Pessoa in his Western Canon.

Yet, Fernando Pessoa is more than one poet. He wrote as several different poets over time, each with their own style, history, interests, and perspectives. There is even influence from one alter-ego - which he called heteronyms - over another. Out of hundreds of heteronyms three are considered "full fledged" by Pessoa scholar, Richard Zenith: Alberto Caeiro, Ricardo Reis, e Alvaro de Campos [1]. Of the three, Caeiro is considered by the other two as their "master."

**Alberto Caeiro and *the Herd Keeper***

Caeiro's masterpiece is *The Herd Keeper*, a collection of 50 poems unified into the theme of his philosophy of sensation and his abhorrence to theory and abstract categories. As such, "The Herd Keeper" embodies Caeiro's poetic philosophy, known as "sensacionismo." Sensacionismo emphasizes the importance of sensory perception and the immediate experience of the world over abstract intellectualism.

---

[1] See https://lithub.com/the-heteronymous-identities-of-fernando-pessoa/

In these opening lines of poem 9, Caeiro introduces the central metaphor of the poem: the poet as the herd keeper, with the herd symbolizing his thoughts. This metaphor underscores the idea that Caeiro's thoughts, like a herd, are simple and natural. He doesn't engage in complex philosophical ponderings but instead embraces the immediacy of sensory experience.

*I'm a herd keeper.*

*The herd is my thoughts*

*And my thoughts are all sensations.*

*I think with my eyes and with my ears*

*And with hands and feet*

*And with the nose and mouth.*

Caeiro continues to emphasize the primacy of the senses in his thinking process. He doesn't rely on abstract reasoning or intellectual analysis; instead, he engages with the world directly through his senses. This direct sensory experience is a fundamental aspect of his *sensacionismo* philosophy.

*To think of a flower is to see and smell it*

*And to eat a fruit is to know its meaning.*

Caeiro suggests that true understanding comes from a direct engagement with the object or idea in question. He uses the example of thinking about a flower by seeing and smelling it. This tactile and sensory approach to thought underscores his rejection of abstract, detached reasoning. To truly understand something, he believes in immersing oneself in the sensory experience of it.

Caeiro paradoxically suggests that while his approach doesn't necessarily yield a structured intellectual understanding of a subject, it allows him to grasp it on a more profound, intuitive level. This aligns with his belief in the importance of immediate sensory experience over abstract analysis.

In "The Herd Keeper," Alberto Caeiro presents a poetic philosophy that celebrates simplicity, direct experience, and the beauty of the natural world. Through his sensory engagement with the world, he invites readers to embrace a more immediate and authentic way of perceiving and understanding life.

Erick Messias

Saint Louis, 2023

# 1

I've never kept herds,
But it is as if I keep them.
My soul is like a shepherd,
It knows the wind and the sun
And walks by the hand of the Seasons
Passing and looking.
All the peace of nature without people
Comes and sits next to me.
But I get sad like a sunset
To our imagination,
When it gets cold at the bottom of the plain
And one can feel night entering
Like a butterfly through the window…

But my sadness is quiet
Because it's natural and fair
And it is what must be in the soul
When it already think it exists
And the hands pick flowers without realizing it....

Like a rattling noise
Beyond the bend in the road,
My thoughts are content.
I only feel sorry to know that they are content,
Because if they didn't know,
Instead of being content and sad,
They would be happy and content.

Thinking is uncomfortable like walking in the rain
When the wind picks up and it seems that it rains more....

I have no ambitions nor desires
Being a poet is not an ambition of mine
It's my way of being alone.

And if I wish sometimes
For imagining, being a little lamb
(Or be the whole herd
To walk spread across the hillside
Being a lot of happy things at the same time),
It's just because I feel what I write at sunset,
Or when a cloud passes its hand over the light
And there runs a silence through the grass…

When I sit down to write verses
Or, walking along the paths or the bypasses,
I write verses on paper that is in my thoughts,
I feel a staff in my hands
And I see a cutout of me
On top of a hill,
Looking at my herd and seeing my ideas
Or looking at my ideas and seeing my herd,
And smiling vaguely as someone who doesn't understand what is being said
And wants to fake understanding…

I salute all who read me,
Tipping off the large hat

When you come to my door
As soon as the stagecoach rises to the top of the hill....
I greet you and wish you sunshine,
And rain, when rain is needed,
And may your houses have
By an open window
a favorite chair
Where you sit, reading my verses.
And when you read my verses, think
That I am anything natural -
For example, the ancient tree
In the shadow of which as children
You sat down with a thud, tired of playing,
And wiped the sweat from the hot brow
With the sleeve of the scratched apron....

# 2

My outlook is clear like a sunflower.
I have the habit of taking walks along the roads
Looking to the left and to the right,
And every now and then looking back...
And what I see every moment
Is something I've never seen before,
And I know how to handle it very well...
I know how to have the essential step
That a child has if, at birth,
Notices that he was really born...
I feel born every moment
For the eternal novelty of the world…

I believe in the world like a marigold,
Because I see it. But I don't think about it
Because to think is to misunderstand...
The world was not made for us to think about it
(To think is to be sick in the eyes)
But for us to look at it and be in agreement....

I don't have a philosophy: I have senses...
If I speak of Nature, it is not because I know what she is,
But because I love her, and I love her for this,
Because those who love never know what they love
Neither why they love, or what it is to love...
Love is eternal innocence,
And the only innocence is not to think…

# 3

At dusk, leaning out the window,
And knowing obliquely that there are fields ahead,
I read until my eyes burn
The book by Cesario Verde[2].

What a pity I have for him!
He was a peasant
That walked imprisoned in freedom through the city.
But the way he looked at the houses,
And the way he observed the streets,
And the way he got on with things,
It's the way of one who looks at trees,
And of one who look down the road they are walking
And he walks around noticing the flowers in the fields...

That's why he had that great sadness
That he never clearly said he had,
But he walked in the city as one walks in the country
And sad as crushing flowers in books
And putting plants in vases...

---

[2] Cesário Verde (1855 – 1886) was a 19th-century Portuguese poet.

# 4

This afternoon the thunderstorm fell
Down the slopes of heaven below
Like a huge boulder...
Like someone who from a high window
Shakes a tablecloth,
And the crumbs, because they all fell together,
Make some noise when falling,
The rain rained down from the sky
And blackened the trails...

When lightning shook the air
And rocked the space
Like a big head that says no,
I don't know why — I wasn't afraid —
I began to pray to Santa Barbara
As if I were someone's old aunt...

Oh! and praying to Santa Bárbara
I felt even simpler
Than I think I am...
I felt familiar and homely
And having gone through life
Quietly, like the backyard wall;
Having ideas and feelings for having them
As a flower has perfume and color...

I felt myself to be someone able to believe in Santa Barbara...

Ah, to be able to believe in Santa Barbara!
(Whoever believes that there is Santa Bárbara,
will judge that she is human and visible
Or what will judge her to be?)

(What a trick! What do
The flowers, the trees, the herds,
Know about Santa Barbara?...
A tree branch,
If it could, could never
Build neither saints nor angels...
It could judge that the sun
Is God, and that the thunderstorm
Is a lot of people
Angry above us...
There, like the simplest of men
Are sick and confused and stupid
Before the clear simplicity
And health in existing
Of trees and plants!)

And I, thinking about all this,
I was again less happy...
I got dark and sick and somber
Like a day when thunder threatens all day
And doesn't come at night.

# 5

There is enough metaphysics in not thinking about anything.

What do I think about the world?
What do I know about what I think about the world!
If I got sick I would think about it.

What idea do I have about things?
What opinion do I have about causes and effects?
What have I meditated on God and the soul
And about the creation of the World?
I don't know. For me to think about this is to close my eyes
And not think. It is to draw the curtains
Of my window (but it has no curtains).

The mystery of things? I don't know what a mystery is!
The only mystery is that there are some who think about the mystery.
Who is under the sun and closes his eyes,
Begins not to know what the sun is
And to think about many things full of heat.
But then the eyes open and see the sun,
And can't think of anything anymore,
Because sunlight is worth more than the thoughts
Of all the philosophers and of all the poets.
Sunlight doesn't know what it's doing

And that's why it doesn't make mistakes and is common and good.

Metaphysics? What metaphysics have those trees
That of being green and leafy and having branches
And that of bearing fruit in its time, which does not make us think,
To us, who don't know how to bear them.
But what better metaphysics than theirs,
That of not knowing what they live for
Not even knowing that they don't know?

'Intimate constitution of things'…
'Intimate sense of the Universe'…
All this is false, all this means nothing.
It's amazing that one can think of such things.
It's like thinking about reasons and ends
When the early morning is breaking, and by the sides of the trees
A vague lustrous gold is losing the darkness.

Thinking about the inner meaning of things
It is adding up, like to think of health
Or to take a glass to the fountains' water.

The only intimate sense of things
It's that they don't have any intimate sense.

I don't believe in God because I've never seen him.
If he wanted me to believe in him,
No doubt he would come talk to me

And he would walk through my door
Saying to me, Here I am!

(This is perhaps ridiculous to the ears
Of those who, not knowing what it is to look at things,
Don't understand who talks about them
With the way of speaking that noticing them teaches.)

But if God is the flowers and the trees
And the hills and sun and the moonlight,
So I believe him,
So I believe him all the time,
And all my life is a prayer and a mass,
And a communion through eyes and ears.

But if God is the trees and the flowers
And the hills and the moonlight and the sun,
Why do I call him God?
I call it flowers and trees and hills and sun and moonlight;
Because, if he has made himself, for me to see him,
Sun and moonlight and flowers and trees and hills,
If he appears to me as trees and hills
And moonlight and sun and flowers,
It is because he wants me to know him
As trees and hills and flowers and moonlight and sun.

And so I obey him,
(What more do I know about God than God about himself?),
I obey him to live, spontaneously,

As one who opens his eyes and sees,
And I call him moonlight and sun and flowers and trees and hills,
And I love him without thinking about him,
And I think of him seeing and hearing,
And I carry him with me all the time.

# 6

To think of God is to disobey God,
Because God wanted us not to know him,
That's why he has not shown himself to us...

Let's be simple and calm,
Like the streams and the trees,
And God will love us by making us
As beautiful as the trees and the streams,
And he will give us lush green in his spring,
And a river to go to when we're done! ...

# 7

From my village I can see as much of the earth as can be seen in the Universe...
That's why my village is as big as any other land
Because I am the size of what I see
And not, the size of my height…

In cities life is smaller
Than here in my house on top of this hill.
In the city the big houses lock the view with a key,
They hide the horizon, push our gaze away from the whole sky,
They make us small because they take away what our eyes can give us,
And they make us poor because our only wealth is seeing.

# 8

At noon, on late spring
I had a dream like a photograph.
I saw Jesus Christ come down to earth.
He came down the side of a hill
Made himself a boy again,
Running and rolling in the grass
And plucking flowers to throw them away
And laughing so as to be heard from afar.

He escaped from heaven.
He was too much of our own to fake
Being the second person of the Trinity.
In heaven everything was false, everything was at odds
With flowers and trees and rocks.
In heaven he had to be serious all the time
And every now and then to become a man again
And climb to the cross, and die forever
With a crown full of thorns
And the feet impaled by a spiked nail,
And even with a rag around the waist
Like the Black people in the illustrations.
They wouldn't even let him have a father and a mother
Like the other kids.
His father was two people
An old man named Joseph, who was a carpenter,
And that he wasn't his father;
And the other father was a stupid dove,
The only ugly dove in the world
Because it was not of the world nor was it a dove.

And his mother hadn't loved before she had him.

She wasn't a woman: she was a suitcase
In which he had come from heaven.
And they wanted him, who had only been born of his mother,
And he never had a father to love with respect,
Preached goodness and justice!

One day when God was sleeping
And the Holy Spirit was flying,
He went to the box of miracles and stole three.
With the first one, he made sure no one knew he had run away.
With the second, he created himself eternally human and child.
With the third he created a Christ eternally on the cross
And he left him nailed to the cross in heaven
So to serve as a model for those.
Then he ran away into the sun
And he went down the first ray he caught.

Today he lives in my village with me.
He is a beautiful child of laughter and nature.
He wipes the nose into the right arm,
Splashes in puddles of water,
Picks flowers and likes them and forgets about them.
He throws stones at donkeys,
Steals the fruit from the orchards
And runs away crying and screaming from the dogs.
And because you know they don't like

And that everyone thinks it's funny,
Runs after girls on the roads
That walk in groups along the roads
with buckets on their heads
And lift their skirts.

He taught me everything.
He taught me how to look at things.
He points me to all the things in the flowers.
Shows me how funny stones are
When we have them at hand
And slowly look at them.

He tells me a lot of awful things about God.
Says he's a sick, stupid old man,
Always spitting on the floor
And saying profanities.
The Virgin Mary spends the afternoons of eternity
making stockings.
And the Holy Spirit scratches himself with his beak
And perches on chairs and gets them dirty.
Everything in heaven is stupid like the Catholic Church.
He tells me that God doesn't understand anything
Of the things he created —
"If he created them at all, which I doubt." —

"He says, for example, that beings sing of his glory,
But the beings do not sing at all.
If they sang they would be singers.
Beings exist and nothing else,
And that is why they are called beings."

And then, tired of speaking ill of God,
Baby Jesus falls asleep in my arms
Where I hold him and I carry him home.

He lives with me in my house in the hills.
He is the Eternal Child, the missing god
He is the human who is natural,
He is the divine who smiles and plays.
And that's why I know for sure
That he is the real Baby Jesus.

And the child, so human that he is divine,
Is my daily life as a poet,
And it's because he's always with me that I'm always a poet.
And that my slightest glance
fills me with sensation,
And the smallest sound, whatever it may be,
seems to speak to me.

The New Child who lives where I live
gives me a hand
And the other hand to everything that exists
And so the three of us go by whatever path there is,
Jumping and singing and laughing
And enjoying our common secret
That is to know everywhere
That there is no mystery in the world
And that it's all worth it.

The Eternal Child always accompanies me.

The direction of my gaze is his pointing finger.
My ear happily listens to every sound
And the tickles he playfully makes in my ears.

We get along so well with each other
In the company of everything
That we never thought about each other,
But we live together and apart
With an intimate agreement
Like right hand and left hand.

At dusk we play five pebbles
On the doorstep of the house,
As befits a god and a poet,
And as if every stone
Were a whole universe
And that was why it was a great danger for it.
To be dropped on the floor.

Then I'll tell him stories about things only men do
And he smiles, because everything is amazing.
Laughing at kings and those who are not kings,
And he is sorry to hear about wars,
And the trades, and the ships
Leaving smoke in the air over the high seas.
Because he knows that all this lacks that truth
That a flower has when it blooms
And that walks with the sunlight
Varying the hills and valleys
And making the whitewashed walls hurt the eyes.

Then he falls asleep and I lay him down.
I carry him inside the house
And I lay him down, undressing him slowly
And as following a very pure ritual
Like a mother until he's naked.

He sleeps inside my soul
And sometimes he wakes up at night
And he plays with my dreams.
He turns some upside down,
Put one on top of the other
And clap his hands alone
Smiling into my sleep.

When I die, little one,
Let me be the child, the smaller one.
Take me in your lap
And take me inside your house.
Undress my tired and human being
And lay me down on your bed.
And tell me stories, in case I wake up,
So that I go back to sleep.
And give me your dreams to play with
Until that day is born
That you know what it is.

This is the story of my Baby Jesus.
Why is it that
It cannot be truer
Than whatever philosophers think
And religions teach?

# 9

I'm a herd keeper.

The herd is my thoughts

And my thoughts are all sensations.

I think with my eyes and with my ears

And with hands and feet

And with the nose and mouth.

To think of a flower is to see and smell it

And to eat a fruit is to know its meaning.

So when on a hot day

I feel sad for enjoying it so much,

And I lie down in the grass,

And I close my warm eyes,

I feel my whole body lying in reality,

I know the truth and I'm happy.

# 10

"Hello, Herd Keeper,

There by the side of the road,

What does the passing wind tell you?"

    "That it is wind, and that passes,

    And that has passed before,

    And that will happen later.

    And what does it say to you?"

"Much more than that,

It tells me about many other things.

Of memories and longing

And of things that never were."

    "You never heard the wind pass.

    The wind only talks about the wind.

    What you heard from the wind was a lie,

    And the lie is in you."

# 11

That lady has a piano

Which is pleasant but it is not the flow of rivers

Nor the murmur that the trees make...


Why do you need a piano?

It is best to have ears

And love nature.

# 12

Virgil's shepherds played flutes and other things

And they sang of love literally.

(After — I never read Virgil.

Why should I read it?)


But Virgil's shepherds, poor things, are Virgil,

And Nature is beautiful and ancient.

# 13

Lightly, lightly, very lightly,

A very lightly wind passes by,

And it goes away, always very lightly.

And I don't know what I think

I don't even try to find out.

# 14

I don't mind the rhymes. Rarely

There are two identical trees, one next to the other.

I think and write as flowers have color

But with less perfection in my way of expressing myself

Because I lack divine simplicity

Of being all just my exterior.


I look and I am moved,

I am moved as water flows when the ground is tilted,

And my poetry is as natural as the rising wind…

# 15

The four songs that follow

Separate from everything I think,

They lie to everything I feel,

They are the reverse of what I am...

I wrote them when I was sick

And that's why they are natural.

And agree with what I feel,

They agree with what they don't agree with...

Being sick I must think otherwise

What I think about when I'm sane.

(Otherwise I wouldn't be sick),

I must feel the opposite of what I feel

When it's me in health,

I must lie to my nature

As a creature that feels a certain way...

I must be all sick—ideas and all.

When I'm sick, I'm not sick for something else.


That's why these songs that deny me

They are not able to disown me

And they are the landscape of my soul at night,

The same in reverse...

# 15a

These four songs, I wrote them when I was sick.

Now they're written down and I don't think about them anymore.

Let us enjoy, if we can, our sickness,

But let's never find health,

As men do.


The fault of men is not that they are sick:

It is to call your disease health,

And that's why they don't seek the cure

Not even really knowing what health and illness are.

# 16

I wish my life was an oxcart

That comes creaking, early in the morning, along the road,

And that where it came from it returns later

Almost at night along the same road.

> I didn't have to get my hopes up — I just had to have wheels...
>
> My old age didn't have wrinkles or gray hair...
>
> When I was no longer fit, they took the wheels off me.
>
> And I was overturned and broken at the bottom of a ravine.

Or else they made me something different

And I didn't know anything about what they were doing to me...

But I'm not a car, I'm different

But how I am really different I would never be told.

# 17

On my plate what a mixture of Nature!

My sisters the plants,

The companions of the fountains, the saints

Who no one prays to...


And they are cut and come to our table

And in hotels the noisy guests,

That arrive with straps having blankets

They ask for «Salad», careless...,

Without thinking that they demand from Mother Earth

Her freshness and her first children,

The first green words she has,

The first living and iridescent things

that Noah saw

When the waters receded and the tops of the mountains

Green and waterlogged

And in the air where the dove appeared

The rainbow faded...

# 18

I wish I was the dust on the road

And that the feet of the poor were trampling me...

I wish I were the flowing rivers

And that the washerwomen were by my side...

I wish I were the poplars by the river

And had only the sky above and the water below. . .

I wish I was the miller's donkey

And that he beat me and cherished me...

Rather that than being who crosses life

Looking back and feeling sorry...

# 19

The moonlight when it hits the grass

I don't know what reminds me...

Reminds me of the voice of the old maid

Telling me fairy tales.

And how Our Lady dressed as a beggar

Walked the roads at night

Helping abused children...


If I can no longer believe that this is true

What does the moonlight hit on the grass for?

# 20 [3]

The Tagus is more beautiful than the river that flows through my village,

But the Tagus is not more beautiful than the river that runs through my village

Because the Tagus is not the river that flows through my village,

The Tagus has big ships

And sails on it still,

For those who see in everything what is not there,

The memory of the caravels.

The Tagus comes from Spain

And the Tagus enters the sea in Portugal.

Everybody knows that.

---

[3] This is one of the most famous poems of Pessoa as Caeiro. It uses the Tagus - the most important river in Portugal to express notions of belonging and being. An American reader might benefit from reading Mississippi where it reads Tagus…

But few know which river is in my village

And where it goes

And where it comes from.

And for that reason, because it belongs to fewer people,

The river in my village is freer and larger.

Through the Tagus you go to the World.

Beyond the Tagus there is America

And the fortune of those who find it.

No one ever thought of what lies beyond

The river in my village.

The river in my village doesn't make you think of anything

Anyone who is near it is only near it.

# 21

If I could crunch the whole earth

And taste it,

And if the earth was a thing to munch on

I would be happier for a moment...

But I don't want to always be happy.

You need to be unhappy from time to time

In order to be natural...

Not everything is sunny days,

And the rain, when scarce, is asked for.

That's why I take unhappiness with happiness

Naturally, as who does not wonder

Let there be mountains and plains

And let there be rocks and grass...

What is needed is to be natural and calm

In happiness or unhappiness,

Feel like someone seeing,

Think like someone who walks,

And when you're going to die, remember that the day dies,

And that the sunset is beautiful and the night that remains is beautiful...

So it is and so be it...

# 22

Like someone who opens the door on a summer day

And is hit by the heat of the fields in his whole face,

Sometimes, all of a sudden, Nature hits me in the face

In the face of my senses,

And I'm confused, disturbed, wanting to understand

I don't know how or what...

But who sent me to want to understand?

Who told me I had to understand?

When summer passes by my face

The light and warm hand of your breeze,

I just have to feel pleasure because it's a breeze

Or to feel unpleasant because it's hot,

And anyway I feel it,

So, because I feel it that way, it is my duty to feel it...

# 23

My gaze is blue like the sky

It is calm like water in the sun.

It is like this, blue and calm,

Because it doesn't question or wonder...


If I interrogated and wonder

No new flowers would bloom in the meadows

Nor would I change anything in the sun to make it more beautiful...

(Even if new flowers bloom in the meadow

And if the sun changed to more beautiful,

I would feel less flowers in the meadow

And I thought the sun was uglier...

Because everything is as it is and that's the way it is,

And I accept, and I don't even thank you,

So I don't seem to think about it...)

# 24

What we see of things are the things.

Why would we see one thing if there was another?

Why seeing and hearing would be deceiving ourselves

If seeing and hearing are seeing and hearing?


The key is knowing how to see,

Knowing how to see without thinking,

Know how to see when you see,

And don't even think about it when you see it,

Not even seeing when thinking.


But that (sad for us who bring our souls dressed!),

That requires in-depth study,

A learning to unlearn

And a kidnapping in the freedom of that convent

That the poets say that the stars are the eternal nuns

And the flowers the penitents convicted of a single day,

But where after all are the stars nothing but stars

Nor the flowers but flowers,

That's why we call them stars and flowers.

# 25

The soap bubbles that this child

Has fun letting go of a straw

They are translucently a whole philosophy.

Clear, useless and fleeting like Nature,


Friends of the eyes like things,

are what they are

With rounded, airy precision,

And no one, not even the child who leaves them,

pretends that they are more than they appear to be.


Some are barely visible in the lucid air.

They are like the breeze that passes by and barely touches the flowers

And that we only know that it passes

Because something is lightened in us

And accepts everything more clearly.

# 26

Sometimes, on days of perfect and exact light,

In which things have all the reality they can have,

I ask myself slowly

Why don't I even attribute

Beauty to things.

Does a flower have beauty?

Does a fruit have beauty?

No: they have color and shape

And existence only.

Beauty is the name of something that doesn't exist

What I give to things in exchange for the pleasure they give me.

It does not mean anything.

So why do I say things: are they beautiful?

Yes, even to me, who live only to live,

Invisible, the lies of men come to me

Faced with things,

In the face of things that simply exist.

How difficult it is to be one's own and not see anything but the visible!

# 27

Only Nature is divine, and it is not divine...

If sometimes I speak of it as a being

It's just that to talk about it I need to use the language of men

That gives personality to things,

And names to things.

But things have no name or personality:

There are, and the sky is large and the earth wide,

And our heart is the size of a closed fist...

Blessed be I for all I don't know.

I enjoy all this like someone who knows there is the sun.

# 28

I read almost two pages today

Of the book of a mystic poet,

And I laughed like someone who has been crying a lot.

Mystic poets are sick philosophers,

And philosophers are crazy men.

Because mystical poets say that flowers feel

And they say that stones have a soul

And that rivers have ecstasies in the moonlight.

But the flowers, if they felt, were not flowers,

They were people;

And if stones had a soul, they were living things, they weren't stones;

And if the rivers had ecstasies in the moonlight,

The rivers would be sick men.

It is necessary not to know what flowers and stones and rivers are

To talk about their feelings.

Talking about the soul of stones, flowers, rivers,

It's talking about yourself and your false thoughts.

Thank God that the stones are only stones,

And that rivers are but rivers,

And that flowers are just flowers.

For myself, I write the prose of my verses

And I'm glad,

Because I know that I understand Nature from the outside;

And I don't understand its inside

Because Nature has no inside;

Otherwise it wasn't Nature.

# 29

I am not always the same in what I say and write.

I change, but I do not change a lot.

The color of the flowers is not the same in the sun

Than when a cloud passes

Or when the night comes

And the flowers are a shade color.

But whoever looks closely sees that they are the same flowers.

So when I seem to disagree with myself,

I suits me:

If I was facing right,

I now turn to the left,

But it's always me, sitting on my feet —

The same always, thanks to heaven and earth

And to my watchful eyes and ears

And to my clear simplicity of soul...

# 30

If you want me to have mysticism, fine, I have it.

I am a mystic, but only with the body.

My soul is simple and does not think.

My mysticism is not wanting to know.

It's living and not thinking about it.

I don't know what Nature is: I sing it.

I live on top of a hill

In a whitewashed and lonely house,

And that's my definition.

# 31

If sometimes I say that flowers smile

And if I say that the rivers sing,

It's not because I think there are smiles in flowers

And songs in the flow of rivers...

It's because that way I make false men better feel

The truly real existence of flowers and rivers.

Because I write for them to read me I sometimes sacrifice

To your stupidity of senses...

I don't agree with me but I absolve myself,

Because I'm just this serious thing, an interpreter of Nature,

Because there are men who don't understand its language,

Because it is not a language.

# 32

Yesterday afternoon a man from the cities

He was speaking at the door of the inn.

He spoke to me too.

He spoke of justice and the fight for justice

And of the suffering workers,

And of constant labor, and of those who are hungry,

And of the rich who only have their backs to them.

And, looking at me, he saw tears in my eyes

And he smiled with pleasure, judging that I felt

The hatred he felt, and the compassion

That he said he felt.

(But I was barely listening to him.

What do men matter to me?

And what do they suffer or suppose they suffer?

Be like me - you will not suffer.

All the evil in the world comes from caring about each other,

Either to do good, or to do evil.

Our soul and heaven and earth are enough for us.

To want more is to miss this, and be unhappy.)

I in what was I thinking

When the friend of the people spoke

(And it moved me to tears),

It was that the distant murmur of rattles

at this dusk

Didn't sound like the bells of a tiny chapel

For the flowers and the streams to go to mass

And simple souls like mine.

(Praise be God I'm no good,

And I have the natural selfishness of flowers

And of the rivers that follow their path

Concentrating without knowing it

In just flowering and flowing.

This is the only mission in the world,

That — to clearly exist,

And knowing how to do it without thinking about it.)


And the man was silent, looking to the west.

But what is the sunset to he who hates and loves?

# 33

Pity those flowers in regular garden beds.

They seem to be afraid of the police...

But so good they are, that they bloom all the same

And they have the same old smile

That they had for the first look of the first man

Who saw them appear and touched them lightly

To see if they spoke...

# 34

I find it so natural that one doesn't think

That I laugh sometimes, alone,

I don't know exactly about what, but it's something

About there being people who think...

What will my wall think of my shadow?

I ask myself this sometimes until I realize

I am asking myself things...

And then I am displeased, and bothered

As if I found myself with a numb foot...

What will this think of that?

Nothing thinks anything.

Is the earth aware of the stones and plants it has?

If she has it, let her have it...

What does it matter to me?

If I thought about these things,

I would stop seeing the trees and plants

And stopped seeing the Earth,

Just to see my thoughts...

Saddened and left in the dark.

And so, without thinking, I have Earth and Heaven.

## 35

The moonlight through the tall branches,

All the poets say that it is more

Than the moonlight through the tall branches.

But for me, who don't know what I think,

What the moonlight through the tall branches

Is, in addition to being

The moonlight through the tall branches,

is not to be anything but

The moonlight through the tall branches.

# 36

And there are poets who are artisans

And they work on their verses

Like a carpenter on boards!...

How sad not to know how to bloom!

Having to put verse on verse, like someone building a wall

And see if it's ok, and remove it if it's not!...

When the only artistic home is the whole Earth

Which changes and is always fine and is always the same.

I think about this, not like someone who thinks, but like someone who breathes.

And I look at the flowers and smile...

I don't know if they understand me

Not even if I understand them,

But I know the truth is in them and in me

And in our common divinity

Of letting go and living for the Earth

And carry in the arms of the happy seasons

And let the wind sing us to sleep

And not having dreams in our sleep.

# 37

Like a big blur of dirty fire

The setting sun lingers in the clouds that remain.

A vague hiss comes from afar in the very calm afternoon.

It must be from a faraway train.

At this moment I have a vague longing

And a vague placid desire

That appears and disappears.

Also sometimes, in the flower of the brooks

Bubbles form in the water

That are born and burst.

And they don't make any sense

Except they are water bubbles

That are born and burst.

# 38

Blessed be the same sun of other lands

That makes my brothers all men

Because all men, for a moment in the day, look at him like I do,

And in that pure moment

All clean and sensitive

return tearfully

And with a sigh they barely feel

To true and primitive man

Who saw the sun rise and still didn't adore it.

Because this is natural — more natural

Than worship gold and God

And art and morals…

# 39

The mystery of things, where is it?

Where is it that does not appear

At least showing us that it's a mystery?

What does the river knows about and what does the tree

And I, who am no more than they, what do I know?

Whenever I look at things and think what men think of them,

I laugh like a brook that sounds cool on a stone.


Because the only hidden meaning of things

Is that they have no hidden meaning,

It's stranger than all oddities

And than the dreams of all poets

And the thoughts of all philosophers,

That things are really what they seem to be

And there is nothing to understand.

Yes, this is what my senses have learned by themselves:—

Things have no meaning: they have existence.

Things are the only hidden meaning of things.

# 40

A butterfly passes before me

And for the first time in the Universe I notice

That butterflies have no color or movement,

Just as flowers have no scent or color.

It is color that has the wings of the butterfly,

In the movement of the butterfly, the movement moves.

Perfume is what has perfume in the perfume of the flower.

The butterfly is just butterfly

And the flower is just flower.

# 41

In the evening of summer days, sometimes

Even though there is no breeze, it seems

That passes, a moment, a light breeze...

But the trees remain still

On every sheet of your sheets

And on our senses had an illusion,

They had the illusion of what would please them...

Ah! the senses, the sick who see and hear!

If only we were as we should be

And there would be no need for illusion in us...

It would be enough for us to feel with clarity and life

And we don't even notice that there are senses...

But thank God there is imperfection in the world

Because imperfection is one thing,

And having people who make mistakes is original,

And having sick people makes the world funny.

If there were no imperfections, there would be one less thing,

And there must be a lot of thing

So we have a lot to see and hear...

# 42

The diligence passed by the road, and went away;

And the road didn't get any prettier, or even uglier.

Thus goes human action around the world.

We take nothing and put nothing; we pass and forget;

And the Sun is always punctual every day.

# 43

Better the flight of the bird, that passes and leaves no trace,

Than the passage of the animal, remembered on the ground.

The bird passes and forgets, and so it should be.

The animal, where it no longer is thus useless,

Shows that it has been, which is of no use.

Remembrance is a betrayal of Nature,

Because yesterday's Nature is not Nature.

What was is nothing, and remembering is not seeing.

Pass, bird, pass, and teach me to pass!

# 44

I wake up suddenly in the night,

And my clock takes up all night.

I don't feel nature out there.

My room is a dark thing with vaguely white walls.

Outside there is a quietness as if nothing exists.

Only the clock continues its noise.

And this little gear thing that's on my desk

It drowns out all existence from heaven and earth ...

I almost get lost thinking what this means,

But I turn around, and I feel myself smile at the corners of my mouth in the night,

Because the only thing my clock symbolizes or means

Filling the enormous night with its smallness

It's the curious feeling of filling the huge night

With its smallness...

And this sensation is curious because only for me does it fill the night

With its smallness…

# 45

A row of trees in the distance, towards the slope.

But what is a row of trees? There are only trees.

Row and the collective of trees are not things, they are names.


Sad of human souls, who put everything in order,

That draw lines from thing to thing,

Who put signs with names on absolutely real trees,

And draw parallels of latitude and longitude

Over the innocent land itself and greener and flowerier than that!

# 46

In this way or that way,

Depending on whether it works or not,

I can sometimes say what I think,

And other times saying it badly and with mixtures,

I go writing my verses without wanting to,

As if writing wasn't something made of gestures,

As if writing were something that happened to me

Like the sun outside.

I try to say what I feel

Without thinking about what I feel.

I try to put the words to the idea

Without needing a hallway

Made of thought to words.

I can't always feel what I know I should feel.

My thought only very slowly swims across the river

Because the suit that men made it wear weighs heavily on him.

I try to strip myself of what I've learned,

I try to forget the way of remembering that I was taught,

And scrape off the paint with which my senses were painted,

Unboxing my true emotions,

Unwrap myself and be me, not Alberto Caeiro,

But a human animal that Nature produced.

And so I write, wanting to feel Nature, not even like a man,

But as someone who feels Nature, and nothing else.

And so I write, sometimes well, sometimes bad,

Sometimes getting what I want to say right, sometimes getting it wrong,

Falling here, getting up there,

But always going my way like a stubborn blind man.

Still, I'm somebody.

I am the Discoverer of Nature.

I am the Argonaut of true sensations.

I bring to the Universe a new Universe

Because I bring to the Universe itself.

This I feel and this I write

Perfectly aware and without not seeing

It's five o'clock in the morning

And that the Sun, which has not yet shown its head

Over the horizon wall,

Even so, one can already see the tips of its fingers

Grabbing the top of the horizon

Wall of low hills.

# 47

On an exceedingly clear day,

Day that made you want to have worked a lot

To not work anything on it,

I glimpsed, like a road through the trees,

What is perhaps the Great Secret,

That Great Mystery of which false poets speak.

I saw that there is no Nature,

That Nature does not exist,

That there are hills, valleys, plains,

That there are trees, flowers, herbs,

That there are rivers and stones,

But that there is no whole to which it belongs,

That a real and true set

Is a disease of our ideas.

Nature is parts without a whole.

This is perhaps the mystery they talk about.

This was what, without thinking or stopping,

I found must be the truth

That everyone is finding and that they don't,

And that only I, because I didn't go to find it, I found it.

# 48

From the highest window of my house

With a white handkerchief I say goodbye

To my verses that leave for humanity

And I'm not happy nor sad.

This is the fate of verses.

I wrote them and I must show them to everyone

Because I can't do otherwise

As the flower cannot hide the color,

Nor the river to hide that flows,

Nor does the tree hide that it bears fruit.

Behold, they are already going far away as in a diligence

And I unintentionally feel sorry

Like a body ache.

Who knows who will read them?

Who knows which hands they will fall into?

Flower, they caught my destiny for their eyes.

Tree, they plucked the fruits for their mouths.

Rio, the destiny of my water was not to stay in me.

I submit and feel almost happy,

Almost happy, like someone who is tired of being sad.

Go away, go away, from me!

The tree passes and is dispersed by Nature.

The flower withers and its dust lasts forever.

The river flows and enters the sea and its water is always the one that was its.

I pass and stay, like the Universe.

# 49

I go inside and close the window.

They bring the lamp and say good night.

And my happy voice says goodnight.

May my life always be this:

The day full of sun, or soft with rain,

Or tempestuous as if the world were ending,

The soft afternoon and the passing ranches

Staring with interest from the window,

The last friendly look given to the tranquility of the trees,

And then, with the window closed, the lamp lit,

Without reading anything, without thinking about anything, or sleeping,

Feeling life flow through me like a river through its bed,

And outside, a great silence like a sleeping god.

## About the authors: Fernando Pessoa - One and Many

By ChatGPT

Fernando Pessoa (1888-1935), born in Lisbon, Portugal, is one of the most enigmatic and influential figures in the world of poetry and literature. He is celebrated for his profound and introspective works, which have left a mark on the literary landscape of the 20th century.

Pessoa's early life was marked by tragedy and loss. At the age of five, he lost his father, and shortly afterward, his family relocated to Durban, South Africa. There, he received an English education, which greatly influenced his writing. Pessoa returned to Portugal in 1905, and his early works reflect the duality of his cultural influences - Portuguese and English.

One of Pessoa's most remarkable literary achievements is the creation of heteronyms, distinct literary personalities with their own styles and perspectives. These heteronyms allowed him to explore diverse themes and emotions within his poetry and prose. The most famous of these heteronyms include Alberto Caeiro, a nature-loving poet; Ricardo Reis, a stoic poet inspired by classicism; Álvaro de Campos, a modernist poet; and Bernardo Soares, the author of "The Book of Disquiet," a deeply introspective and philosophical work.

Throughout his life, Pessoa's writings delved into themes of identity, existence, and the multifaceted nature of reality. His works, often characterized by their melancholic and existential tone, resonate with readers and critics alike. His poetry is marked by its introspection and exploration of the human condition, reflecting the uncertainty and flux of modern life.

Pessoa's literary career was not limited to poetry. He was an accomplished essayist, translator, and critic, contributing significantly to Portuguese literature. Despite his literary talents, Pessoa lived a relatively reclusive life, working as a freelance translator and collaborating with various literary magazines.

Pessoa died on November 30, 1935, at the age of 47, due to cirrhosis of the liver. In death, he left behind a treasure trove of unpublished works, which continue to be discovered and published to this day.

Fernando Pessoa's legacy endures through his profound and innovative body of work, which has inspired generations of poets and writers around the world. His ability to navigate the complexities of human existence and his unique approach to literature have solidified his place as one of Portugal's most celebrated literary figures and a global literary icon.

## About the authors: Alberto Caeiro, the Poetic Sage of Simplicity

By ChatGPT

Alberto Caeiro, one of the most distinctive and influential heteronyms created by Portuguese poet Fernando Pessoa, was born in Lisbon, Portugal, on April 16, 1889, although this date is a fictional construct given by Pessoa. Caeiro is celebrated for his unique and unconventional approach to poetry, which stood in stark contrast to the prevailing literary trends of his time.

Caeiro's life, as imagined by Pessoa, was characterized by a deep connection to nature and an uncompromising pursuit of simplicity and authenticity. He lived in the countryside of Portugal, where he worked as a shepherd, an occupation that allowed him to immerse himself in the natural world that would become the central theme of his poetry.

Caeiro's poetic philosophy, known as "sensacionismo," revolved around the idea that the only reality we can know is the reality of our sensory perceptions. He rejected metaphysical abstractions and intellectual musings in favor of the immediate and unadulterated experience of the world. His poems often celebrate the beauty of nature, the significance of everyday moments, and the wisdom of living in harmony with the rhythms of the natural world.

One of Caeiro's most famous works is the collection of poems titled "The Herd Keeper" ("O Guardador de Rebanhos"), where he explores his philosophical ideas through the voice of a shepherd. In these poems, he emphasizes the importance of living in the present moment, celebrating the simplicity of existence, and embracing the direct experience of life.

Caeiro's poetry is characterized by its clarity and simplicity, often written in a free-verse style that eschews traditional rhyme and meter. His work had a profound influence on modernist poetry, particularly the poetry of Fernando Pessoa's other heteronyms/poets like Álvaro de Campos and Ricardo Reis.

Despite his relatively short life, Alberto Caeiro's impact on literature has been enduring. He passed away in Pessoa's literary universe, but his poetic legacy continues to inspire readers and writers, inviting them to contemplate the beauty and wisdom of the natural world and the profound simplicity of existence. Caeiro remains a testament to Pessoa's creative genius and his ability to breathe life into multiple literary personas, each with its own unique perspective on the human experience.

## About this translation

This translation is my own version of Pessoa's poems revisiting verses stuck in my memory for over 50 years - half lived in Brazil/Portuguese, half lived in the US/English. It is written for my American English children and friends.

Paraphrasing Pessoa in the closing lines of The Herd Keeper poem 8:

*This is the story of my Fernando Pessoa.*
*Why is it that*
*It cannot be truer*
*Than whatever other translators think*
*And academics teach?*


Erick Messias is a Brazilian American physician and translator.

Printed in Dunstable, United Kingdom